T0266035

The Crowning Glory

NEW DESCANTS
FOR CHURCH CHOIRS

CHURCH PUBLISHING
an imprint of
Church Publishing Incorporated, New York

TABLE OF CONTENTS

INTRODUCTION

The origin of the descant, which means "singing apart", can be traced to an initial development of a second part added above a plainsong melody as early as the 11th century in Europe. It continued to evolve and flourish through the 14th and 15th centuries with the practice of improvising a "discant" against a plainsong melody following strict rules of harmonic relationship. Today's practice of adding a countermelody to the unison singing of a congregational hymn can perhaps create as much delight to our overburdened ears as did the addition of the discant to plainsong centuries ago.

In this new collection of descants, the hymn numbers and first lines preceding the music of each descant refer to *The Hymnal 1982* of the Episcopal Church and, in a few cases, to *Wonder, Love, and Praise* and *Lift Every Voice and Sing II*. These descants may be adapted for use with hymns in other denominational hymnals. The composers have indicated which stanza of the hymn should be accompanied by the descant. In some cases they have noted that the descant could be sung with other stanzas or even other texts. In the layout of this book, some pages have intentionally been left blank to avoid unnecessary page turns for the singer.

Although descants are often reserved mostly for the final stanza of joyous, festive hymns, there are also several in this volume that accompany quieter, more introspective hymns such as those on the tunes *Detroit, Decatur Place,* and *Le Cénacle.* Many descants here could be played alternatively by an instrument, often a trumpet. (See *Antioch* by Gordon King and Cwm Rhondda by William Bradley Roberts, as well as others.). Some of the descants feature two parts such as *Salve festa dies* by Douglas C. Shambo II and *Pleading Savior* by Thomas Pavlechko. Others are written in combination with alternate harmonizations of the hymn tune. (See *St. Clement* by Richard Webster and *Rockville* by Thaddeus P. Cavuoti.)

These descants, harvested from working Episcopal church musicians, are examples of the useful day-to-day work in the local congregation. Such practical compositions rarely capture the attention beyond the local parish, other than being shared with a few close colleagues of the composer. The theme of the 2005 Annual Conference of the Association of Anglican Musicians in Baltimore, Maryland, was "Come to us, Creative Spirit: The Art and Craft of the Church Musician." The vision embodied in the title of the David Mowbray hymn ("Come to us, creative Spirit") is one honoring the creativity of those who speak their faith artistically and seeks to make such voices available to all. It is in that spirit that this book of descants is published.

Abbot's Leigh

Cyril Vincent Taylor (b. 1907-1991)

523 Glorious things of thee are spoken, stanza 4

4 Blest in- Blest in - hab - it - ants of Zi - on, washed in the Re -
deem - er's blood! Je - sus Je - sus, whom souls re - ly on,
makes them kings and priests to God. 'Tis his His love peo - ple
rais - es o - ver o - ver self to reign as kings: and as
and as priests, his sol - emn prais - es each an of - fering brings.

Words: John Newton (1725-1807), alt.
Descant: William Bradley Roberts © 1996 William Bradley Roberts. All rights reserved. Used by permission.

Aberystwyth

Joseph Parry (1841-1903)

699 Jesus, Lover of my soul, stanza 3

3 Plen-teous grace with thee is found, grace_____ to cleanse from ev - ery sin;

let the heal - ing streams a-bound, make_____ and keep me pure with-in. Thou_____

_____ of life the foun - tain art, free - ly let me take of thee: spring_____

_____ thou up with - in my heart, rise_____ to all e - ter - ni - ty.

Words: Charles Wesley (1707-1788), alt.
Descant: William Bradley Roberts © 2003 William Bradley Roberts. Used by permission. All rights reserved.

Aberystwyth

Joseph Parry (1841-1903)

640 Watchman, tell us of the night, stanza 2
699 Jesus, Lover of my soul, stanza 3

beams a - lone gild the spot that gave them birth?
foun - tain art, free - ly let me take of thee:

Trav - 'ler, a - ges are its own;
spring thou up with - in my heart,

see, it bursts o'er all the earth.
rise to all e - ter - ni - ty.

Words: (640) John Bowring (1792-1872) (699) Charles Wesley (1707-1788), alt.
Desc. and harm.: Richard R. Webster © 2002 Richard R. Webster. Used by permission. All rights reserved.

Antioch

George Frideric Handel (1685-1759)

100 Joy to the world!, stanza 4

4 He rules the world with truth and grace, and makes the na - tions prove the glo - ries of his right - eous - ness, and won - ders of O sing, and won - ders of O sing and won - ders and won - ders of his love.

Antioch

George Frideric Handel (1685-1759)

100 Joy to the world!, stanza 4

4 He rules the world with truth and grace, and makes the na - tions prove the glo - ries, glo - ries of his right - eous - ness and won - ders of his love, and won - ders of his love, the won - ders of his love.

Aurelia

Samuel Sebastian Wesley (1818-1876)

525 The Church's one foundation, stanza 5

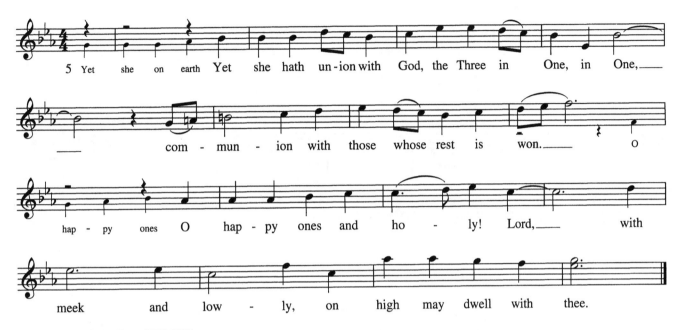

5 Yet she on earth Yet she hath un-ion with God, the Three in One, in One,___ ___ com-mun-ion with those whose rest is won.___ O hap-py ones O hap-py ones and ho-ly! Lord,___ with meek and low-ly, on high may dwell with thee.

Words: Samuel John Stone (1839-1900)
Descant: William Bradley Roberts © 2002 William Bradley Roberts. Used by permission. All rights reserved.

Austria

Franz Joseph Haydn (1732-1807)

522 Glorious things of thee are spoken, stanza 4

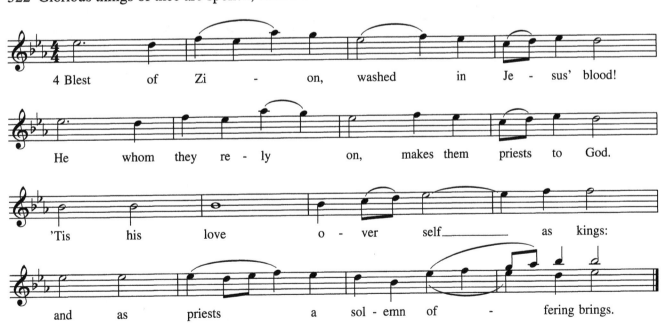

4 Blest of Zi-on, washed in Je-sus' blood! He whom they re-ly on, makes them priests to God. 'Tis his love o-ver self___ as kings: and as priests a sol-emn of-fering brings.

Words: John Newton (1725-1807), alt.
Descant: Jack Warren Burnam © 1997 Jack Warren Burnam. Used by permission. All rights reserved.

Bingham

Dorothy Howell Sheets (b. 1915) © 1984 Dorothy Howell Sheets

585 Morning glory, starlit sky

Ah_____ Ah_____

Ah_____

Birmingham

from *Repository of Sacred Music, Part II, 1813*

437 Tell out, my soul, stanza 4

4 Tell out, my soul, the glo - ries of his word! Firm
is his Firm pro - mise and his mer - cies sure.
Tell out, my soul Tell out the great - ness of the Lord
to chil - dren's chil - dren and for ev - er - more!

Bromley

Franz Joseph Haydn (1732-1809)

29   O Trinity of blessed light, stanza 3

May also be used with hymn #28 "O blest Creator"

Words: Charles Coffin (1676-1749); tr. John Chandler (1806-1876)
Desc. and harm.:   Richard R. Webster © 1988 Richard R. Webster. Used by permission. All rights reserved.

Brother James' Air

J.L. Macbeth Bain (1840?-1925)

517 How lovely is thy dwelling-place, stanza 4

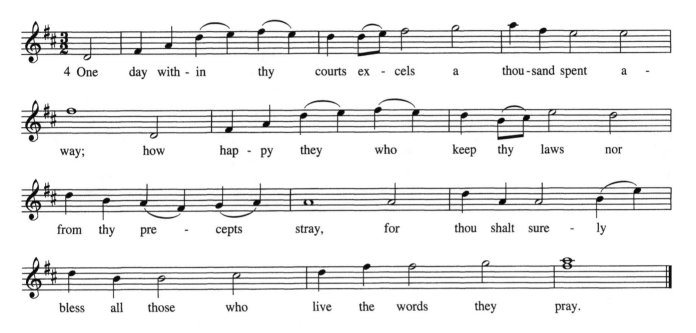

4 One day with-in thy courts ex - cels a thou-sand spent a -
way; how hap - py they who keep thy laws nor
from thy pre - cepts stray, for thou shalt sure - ly
bless all those who live the words they pray.

Words: Carl P. Daw, Jr. (b. 1944) © 1982 Carl P. Daw, Jr. Used by permission. All rights reserved.
Descant: William Bradley Roberts © 2002 William Bradley Roberts. Used by permission. All rights reserved.

Carlisle

Charles Lockhart (1745-1815)

138 All praise to you, O Lord, stanza 4

4 So, led from strength to strength, grant us, O Lord, O Lord, to see the mar - riage sup - per of the Lamb, the great e - piph - a - ny.

Words:　　　Hyde W. Beadon (1812-1891), alt.
Desc. and harm.: Richard R. Webster © 2002 Richard R. Webster. Used by permission. All rights reserved.

Coronation

Oliver Holden (1765-1844)

450 All hail the power of Jesus' Name!, stanza 6

6 Let ev - ery kin - dred, ev - ery tribe, on this ter - res - trial ball, to him all ma - jes - ty as - cribe, and crown him Lord of all! To him all ma - jes - ty as - cribe, and crown him Lord of all!

Cwm Rhondda

John Hughes (1873-1932)

594 God of grace and God of glory, stanza 4

4 Save us from weak res - ig - na - tion to the e - vils we de - plore; let the gift of thy sal - va - tion be our glo - ry ev - er - more. Grant us wis - dom, grant us cou - rage, serv - ing thee whom we a - dore, serv - ing thee whom we a - dore.

Cwm Rhondda

John Hughes (1873-1932)

594 God of grace and God of glory, stanza 4
690 Guide me, O thou great Jehovah, stanza 3

594 4 Save us from weak res-ig-na-tion to the e-vils we de-plore;
690 3 When I tread the verge of Jor-dan, bid my anx-ious fears sub-side;

let the gift of thy sal-va-tion be our glo-ry ev-er-more.
death of death, and hell's de-struc-tion, land me safe on Ca-naan's side;

Grant us wis-dom, grant us cou-rage, serv-ing thee whom
songs of prais-es, songs of prais-es, I will ev-er

we a-dore, ser-ving thee whom we a-dore.
give to thee, I will ev-er give to thee.

Words: (594) Harry Emerson Fosdick (1878-1969), alt.   (690) William Williams (1717-1791); tr. Peter Williams (1722-1796), alt.
Desc. and harm.: Thaddeus P. Cavuoti © 1985 Thaddeus P. Cavuoti. Used by permission. All rights reserved.

Decatur Place

Richard Wayne Dirksen (1921-2003) © 1984 Richard W. Dirksen

51   We the Lord's people, stanza 3

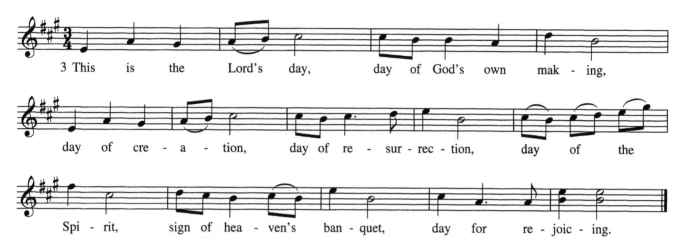

3 This is the Lord's day, day of God's own mak - ing,
day of cre - a - tion, day of re - sur - rec - tion, day of the
Spi - rit, sign of hea - ven's ban - quet, day for re - joic - ing.

Detroit

from *Supplement to Kentucky Harmony, 1820*

674   "Forgive our sins as we forgive," stanza 4

4 Lord, cleanse the depths with - in our souls, and bid re - sent - ment cease; then,
re - con - ciled to God and man, our lives will spread your peace.

Deus tuorum militum

from *Antiphoner, 1753*

448 O love, how deep, how broad, how high, stanza 6

6 All glo - ry to our Lord and God for love so deep, so

high, so broad; the Trin - i - ty whom we a -

dore for ev - er and for ev - er - more.

Words: Latin, 15th cent.; tr. Benjamin Webb (1819-1885), alt.
Descant.: William Bradley Roberts © 2002 William Bradley Roberts. Used by permission. All rights reserved.

Diademata

George Job Elvey (1816-1893)

494 Crown him with many crowns, stanza 1

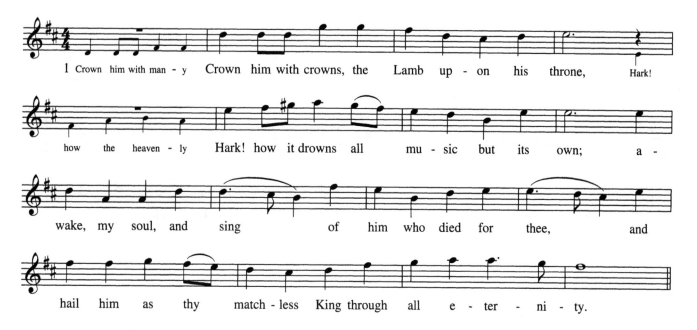

1 Crown him with man - y Crown him with crowns, the Lamb up - on his throne, Hark!

how the heaven - ly Hark! how it drowns all mu - sic but its own; a -

wake, my soul, and sing of him who died for thee, and

hail him as thy match - less King through all e - ter - ni - ty.

Words: Matthew Bridges (1800-1894)
Descant: Gordon King © 1969 Gordon King. Used by permission. All rights reserved.

Down Ampney

Ralph Vaughan Williams (1872-1958) © Oxford University Press

516 Come down, O Love divine, stanza 3

Love cre - ate a place where - in the

Ho - ly Spi - rit makes a dwell - ing.

Words: Bianco da Siena (d. 1434?); tr. Richard Frederick Littledale (1833-1890), alt.
Desc. and harm.: Richard R. Webster © 2002 Richard R. Webster. Used by permission. All rights reserved.

Down Ampney

Ralph Vaughan Williams (1872-1958) © Oxford University Press

516 Come down, O Love divine, stanza 3

3 And so the yearn-ing strong, with which the soul____ will long, shall far____ out-pass the power of hu-man tell-ing; for none can guess its for none can guess its grace, till Love cre-ate a place where-in the Ho-ly Spi-rit dwell-ing.

Words: Bianco da Siena (d. 1434?); tr. Richard Frederick Littledale (1833-1890), alt.
Descant: William Bradley Roberts © 1995 William Bradley Roberts. Used by permission. All rights reserved.

Duke Street

John Hatton (d. 1793)

544 Jesus shall reign, stanza 5

5 Let ev-ery crea-ture rise and bring pe-cu-liar hon-ors to our, to our King; an-gels de-scend with songs a-gain, and earth re-peat the loud a-men: A-men!

Words: Isaac Watts (1674-1748), alt.
Descant: William Bradley Roberts © 2004 William Bradley Roberts. Used by permission. All rights reserved.

Dundee

from *The CL Psalmes of David*, 1615

526 Let saints on earth in concert sing, stanza 5

709 O God of Bethel, by whose hand, stanza 5. Use only the harmonization for either hymn 526 or 126
   from *The Hymnal 1982*.

126 The people who in darkness walked, stanza 5

526 5 Je - sus, be thou our con - stant Guide; then, when the word is given,
709 5 Such bless - ings from thy gra - cious hand our hum - ble prayers im - plore;
126 5 His power in - creas - ing still shall spread, his reign no end shall know;

bid Jor - dan's nar - row stream di - vide, and bring us safe to heaven.
and thou shalt be our cov - enant God and por - tion ev - er - more.
and jus - tice guard his throne a - bove, and peace a - bound be - low.

Words: Charles Wesley (1707-1788), alt.
Descant: Thaddeus P. Cavuoti © 2004 Thaddeus P. Cavuoti. Used by permission. All rights reserved.

Dunedin

Vernon Griffiths (1894-1985)

31   Most Holy God, the Lord of heaven, stanza 5
455 O Love of God, how strong and true, stanza 4
779 *Wonder, Love, and Praise* The church of Christ in every age, stanza 5

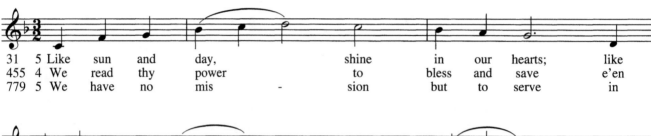

31 5 Like sun and day, shine in our hearts; like
455 4 We read thy power to bless and save e'en
779 5 We have no mis - sion but to serve in

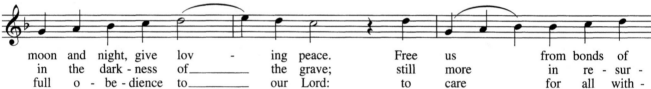

moon and night, give lov - ing peace. Free us from bonds of
in the dark - ness of_____ the grave; still more in re - sur -
full o - be - dience to_____ our Lord: to care for all with -

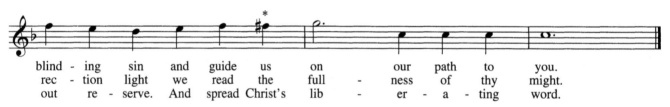

blind - ing sin and guide us on our path to you.
rec - tion light we read the full - ness of thy might.
out re - serve. And spread Christ's lib - er - a - ting word.

When using F♯, alter the Hymnal 1982 harmony to agree.

Words: (31) Latin; tr. Ann K. LeCroy (b. 1930)   (455) Horatius Bonar (1808-1889)
         (779) Fred Pratt Green (1903-2000) © 1971 Hope Publishing Co., Carol Stream, IL 60188.
Descant: Larry D. Cook © 2001 Larry D. Cook. Used by permission. All rights reserved.

Dunedin

Vernon Griffiths (1894-1985)

455 O Love of God, how strong and true*

We read thy power We read thy power_____ to bless and save_____ e'en in the dark - ness of the grave;_____ still more in re - sur - rec - tion light we read the full - ness of thy might.

This descant may accompany any stanza of any text set to this tune.

Words: Horatius Bonar (1808-1889)
Descant: David G. Kelley © 2004 David G. Kelley. Used by permission. All rights reserved.

Dunedin

Vernon Griffiths (1894-1985)

779 *Wonder, Love, and Praise* The church of Christ in every age, stanza 5
455 O Love of God, how strong and true, stanza 4

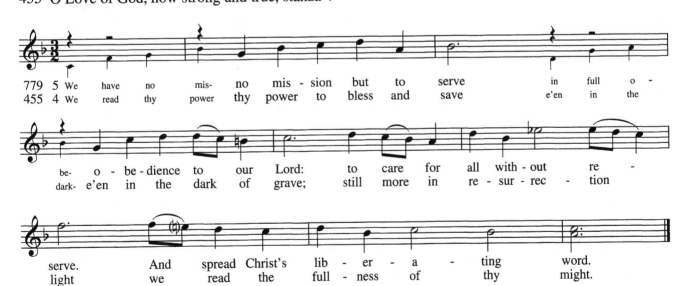

779 5 We have no mis- no mis - sion but to serve in full o -
455 4 We read thy power thy power to bless and save e'en in the

be - o - be - dience to our Lord: to care for all with - out re -
dark- e'en in the dark of grave; still more in re - sur - rec - tion

serve. And spread Christ's lib - er - a - ting word.
light we read the full - ness of thy might.

Words: (779) Fred Pratt Green (1903-2000) © 1971 Hope Publishing Co., Carol Stream, IL 60188. (455) Horatius Bonar (1808-1889)
Descant.: William Bradley Roberts © 2002 William Bradley Roberts. Used by permission. All rights reserved.

Dunedin

Vernon Griffiths (1894-1985)

455 O Love of God, how strong and true, stanza 4

4 We read thy power to bless and save e'en in the
dark - ness of the grave; in re - sur - rec - tion
light we read the full - ness of thy might.

Words: Horatius Bonar (1808-1889)
Descant: Thaddeus P. Cavuoti © 1999 Thaddeus P. Cavuoti. Used by permission. All rights reserved.

Earth and All Stars

David N. Johnson (1922-1987) © Augsburg Fortress Publishing

412 Earth and all stars, stanza 6

6 Know - ledge and Know - ledge and truth, loud wis - dom, sing to the
Lord_____ a new song! Daugh-ter and son, loud pray-ing mem - bers,
sing to the Lord_____ a new song! He has done mar -
- ve - lous things._____ I, too, will praise him with a new_____ song!

Words: Herbert F. Brokering (b. 1926)
Descant: William Bradley Roberts © 2004 William Bradley Roberts. Used by permission. All rights reserved.

Easter Hymn

from *Lyra Davidica*, 1708; adapt. *The Compleat Psalmodist*, 1749

207 Jesus Christ is risen today, stanza 4

4 Sing we to our God above, Alleluia!
praise eternal as his love, Alleluia!
all ye heavenly host, Alleluia!
Father, Son, and Holy Ghost. Alleluia!

Words: Charles Wesley (1707-1788)
Desc. and harm.: Thaddeus P. Cavuoti © 2000 Thaddeus P. Cavuoti. Used by permission. All rights reserved.

Ellers

Edward John Hopkins (1818-1901)

345 Savior, again to thy dear Name we raise, stanza 4

4 Thy peace in Thy peace in life, the balm of ev - ery pain; thy peace, the hope to rise a - gain; then, when our con - flict cease, call us, O Lord, to thy peace.

Words: John Ellerton (1826-1893), alt.
Desc. and harm.: Thaddeus P. Cavuoti © 1993 Thaddeus P. Cavuoti. Used by permission. All rights reserved.

Engelberg

Charles Villiers Stanford (1852-1924)

420 When in our music God is glorified, stanza 5

5 Ah_____
Ah_____ Ah_____
___ Al - le - lu - ia! Al - le - lu - ia! A - men.

Evening Hymn

Gerald Near (b. 1942)

37 O brightness of the immortal Father's face, stanza 3

3 Worth - y art thou at all times to re - ceive our hal - lowed
prais - es, Lord. O Son of God, be thou, in
whom we live, through_____ all the world a - dored.

Lower part is optional.

Words: Greek, 3rd cent.; tr. Edward W. Eddis (1825-1905)

Eventide

William Henry Monk (1823-1889)

662 Abide with me: fast falls the eventide, stanza 4

Words: Henry Francis Lyte (1793-1847)
Desc. and harm.: Thaddeus P. Cavuoti © 1992 Thaddeus P. Cavuoti. Used by permission. All rights reserved.

Festal Song

William H. Walter (1825-1893)

551 Rise up, ye saints of God, stanza 3

3 Lift high the cross of Christ! Tread where his feet have trod; and
quick - ened by the Spi - rit's power, rise up, ye saints of God!

Words: William Pierson Merrill (1867-1954), alt. Used by permission of The Presbyterian Outlook, Richmond, VA.
Descant: William Bradley Roberts © 2002 William Bradley Roberts. Used by permission. All rights reserved.

Finnian

Christopher Dearnley (b. 1930) © Oxford University Press

492 Sing, ye faithful, sing with gladness, stanza 4

4 Now on high, ev - er with us, from his Fa - ther's throne the Son
rules and guides the world he ran - somed, till the ap -point - ed work be done,
till he see, re - newed and per - fect
all things gath - ered in - to one.

Words: John Ellerton (1826-1893), alt.
Descant: Albert Campbell © 2004 Albert Campbell. Used by permission. All rights reserved.

Finnian

Christopher Dearnley (b. 1930) © Oxford University Press

506 Praise the Spirit in creation, stanza 6
492 Sing, ye faithful, sing with gladness, stanza 4

506 6 Praise, O Praise, O Praise the Spi - rit, praise the Fa - ther, praise the

492 4 Now on Now on high, yet ev - er with us, from his Fa - ther's throne the

Word, In - spi - ra - tion, Tri - ni - ty in deep ac - cord;

Son guides the world he ran - somed, till th'ap - point - ed work be done,

through your voice which speaks with - in us,_____ we call you Lord.

till he see, re - newed and per - fect, all gath - ered in - to one.

Words: (506) Michael Hewlett (b. 1916), alt. © Oxford University Press. Used by permission. All rights reserved.
         (492) John Ellerton (1826-1893), alt.
Desc. and harm.: Thaddeus P. Cavuoti © 1997 Thaddeus P. Cavuoti. Used by permission. All rights reserved.

Forest Green

English melody

705 As those of old their first fruits brought, stanza 3

3 With grat - i -tude and hum - ble trust we bring our best to thee to

serve thy cause and share thy love with all hu - man - i - ty. O

thou who gav - est us thy - self in Je - sus Christ thy Son, help

us to give our - selves each day un - til life's work is done.

Words: Frank von Christierson (b. 1900), alt. © 1961 The Hymn Society of America. Used by permission. All rights reserved.
Descant: Susan B. Stiller © 1999 Susan B. Stiller. Used by permission. All rights reserved.

Gloria

French carol

96   Angels we have heard on high, refrain

Gloria

French carol

96   Angels we have heard on high, refrain

Grid

Thomas Pavlechko (b. 1962)

753 *Wonder, Love, and Praise* When from bondage we are summoned, stanza 5

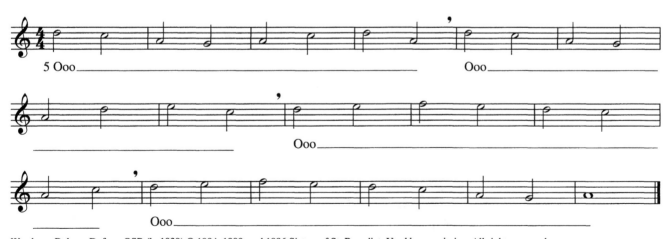

Hanover

att. William Croft (1678-1727)

388 O worship the King, all glorious above, stanza 5

5 Frail child-ren of dust, and fee-ble as frail,_____ we
trust, nor find thee, nor find thee to fail; thy mer-cies, how
ten-der! how firm to the end! Our Ma-ker, Re-deem-er, and Friend!

Words: Robert Grant (1779-1838)
Descant: Douglas C. Shambo II © 1999 Douglas C. Shambo II. Used by permission. All rights reserved.

Hanover

att. William Croft (1678-1727)

388 O worship the King, all glorious above, stanza 5

5 Frail chil-dren of dust, fee-ble, frail,
thee we trust, nor find thee to fail;
thy mer-cies, how firm to the end! Our
Ma-ker, De-fen-der, Re-deem-er, and Friend!

Words: Robert Grant (1779-1838)
Descant: Richard Clemmitt © 2004 Richard Clemmitt. Used by permission. All rights reserved.

Helmsley

Thomas Augustine Arne (1710-1778)

57   Lo! he comes, with clouds descending, stanza 4

4 Yea, a - men! let all a - dore thee, high on
thine e - ter - nal throne; Sa - vior, take the
power and glo - ry; claim the king - dom for thine own:
Al - le - lu - ia!_____ Al - le - lu - ia!
Al - le - lu - ia! Thou shalt reign, and thou a - lone.

Words: Charles Wesley (1707-1788)
Descant: Albert Campbell © 2004 Albert Campbell. Used by permission. All rights reserved.

Hyfrydol

Rowland Hugh Prichard (1811-1887)

657 Love divine, all loves excelling, stanza 3*

3 Fi - nish then thy new cre - a - tion; pure and spot - less
let us be; let us see thy great sal - va - tion
per - fect - ly re - stored in thee: changed from

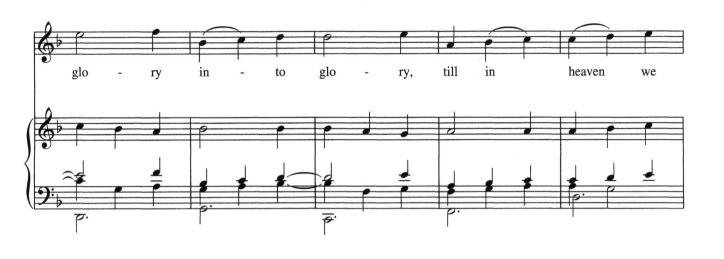

glo - ry in - to glo - ry, till in heaven we

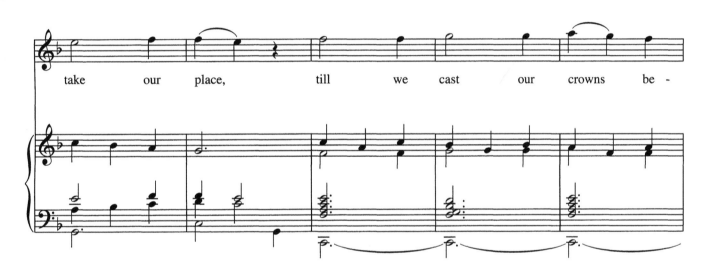

take our place, till we cast our crowns be -

fore thee, lost in won - der, love, and praise.

*This descant may accompany any stanza of any text set to this tune

Words: Charles Wesley (1707-1788)

Hyfrydol

Rowland Hugh Prichard (1811-1887)

460 Alleluia! sing to Jesus!, stanza 5

5 Al - le - lu - ia! sing to Je - sus! his the scep - ter
  Al - le - lu - ia! his the tri - umph, his the vic - to -

his the throne; Hark! the songs of ho - ly Zi - on
ry a - lone;

thun - der like a might - y flood; Je - sus out of

ev - ery na - tion hath re - deemed us by his blood.

Words: William Chatterton Dix (1837-1898)
Descant: Douglas C. Shambo II © 2000 Douglas C. Shambo II. Used by permission. All rights reserved.

Hyfrydol

Rowland Hugh Prichard (1811-1887)

460 Alleluia! sing to Jesus! any stanza*

Al - - - le - lu - ia!_____

_____ Al - le - lu - ia!

Al - le - lu - ia! Al - le - lu - ia! Al - le - lu - ia!_____

*May be played on trumpet

Words: William Chatterton Dix (1837-1898)

Hyfrydol

Rowland Hugh Prichard (1811-1887)

460 Alleluia! sing to Jesus!, stanza 5

5 Al - le - lu - ia! Al - le - lu - ia!____ his the scep - ter,
his the throne; Al - le - lu - ia! Al - le - lu - ia!____ his the
vic - to - ry a - lone; Hark! the songs of ho - ly
Zi - on thun - der like a might - y flood; Je - sus out of
ev - ery na - tion hath re - deemed us by his blood.

Words: William Chatterton Dix (1837-1898)
Descant: Harold W. Friedell © 1996 Pine Hill Press. Used by permission. All rights reserved.

King's Weston

Ralph Vaughan Williams (1872-1958) © Oxford University Press

435 At the Name of Jesus, stanza 6

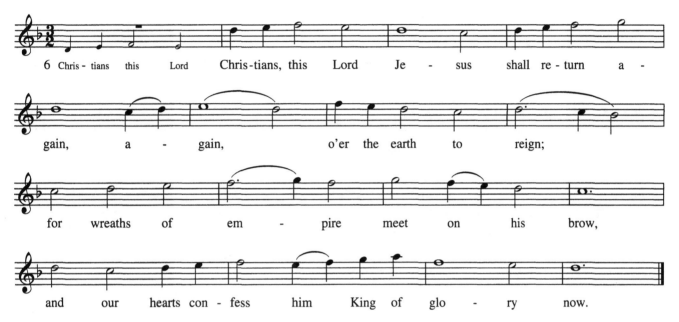

6 Chris - tians this Lord Chris - tians, this Lord Je - sus shall re - turn a -
gain, a - gain, o'er the earth to reign;
for wreaths of em - pire meet on his brow,
and our hearts con - fess him King of glo - ry now.

Words: Caroline Maria Noel (1817-1877), alt.
Descant: Gordon King © 2004 Gordon King. Used by permission. All rights reserved.

Lambillotte

Louis Lambillotte, SJ (1796-1855)

112 *Lift Every Voice and Sing* Come, Holy Ghost, Creator blest, stanza 4

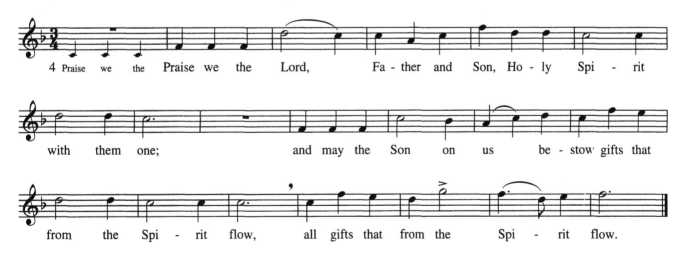

4 Praise we the Praise we the Lord, Fa - ther and Son, Ho - ly Spi - rit
with them one; and may the Son on us be - stow gifts that
from the Spi - rit flow, all gifts that from the Spi - rit flow.

Words: attr. Rabanus Maurus, (776-856); tr. Edward Caswell (1814-1878), alt.
Descant: Thomas Pavlechko © 2004 Thomas Pavlechko. Used by permission. All rights reserved.

Lancashire

Henry Thomas Smart (1813-1879)

563 Go forward, Christian soldier, stanza 4

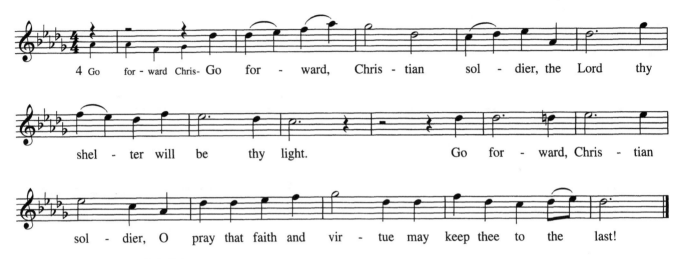

4 Go forward Chris- Go for - ward, Chris - tian sol - dier, the Lord thy
shel - ter will be thy light. Go for - ward, Chris - tian
sol - dier, O pray that faith and vir - tue may keep thee to the last!

Land of Rest

American folk melody

304 I come with joy to meet my Lord, stanza 5
620 Jerusalem, my happy home, stanza 5

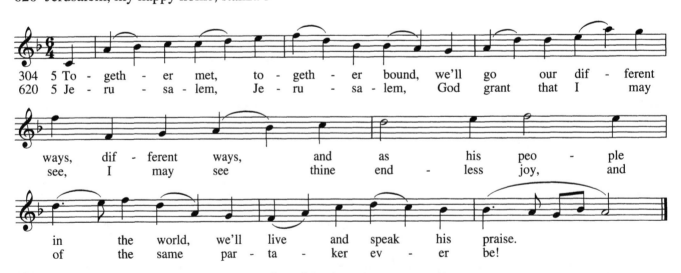

304 5 To - geth - er met, to - geth - er bound, we'll go our dif - ferent
620 5 Je - ru - sa - lem, Je - ru - sa - lem, God grant that I may

ways, dif - ferent ways, and as his peo - ple
see, I may see thine end - less joy, and

in the world, we'll live and speak his praise.
of the same par - ta - ker ev - er be!

Langham

Geoffrey Turton Shaw (1879-1943). Used by permission of the United Nations Association

573 Father eternal, Ruler of creation, stanza 5

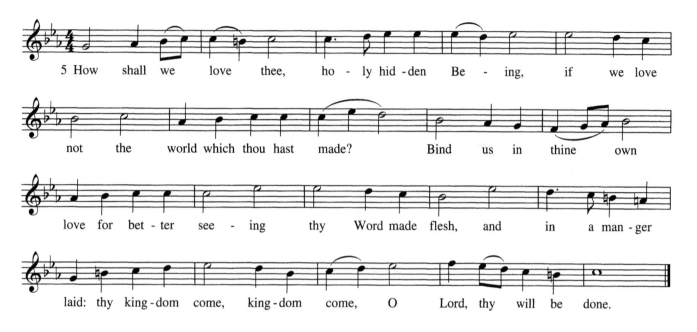

5 How shall we love thee, ho - ly hid - den Be - ing, if we love
not the world which thou hast made? Bind us in thine own
love for bet - ter see - ing thy Word made flesh, and in a man - ger
laid: thy king - dom come, king - dom come, O Lord, thy will be done.

Lasst uns erfreuen

melody from *Auserlesene Catholische Geistliche Kirchengeseng*, 1623

400 All creatures of our God and King, stanza 7*

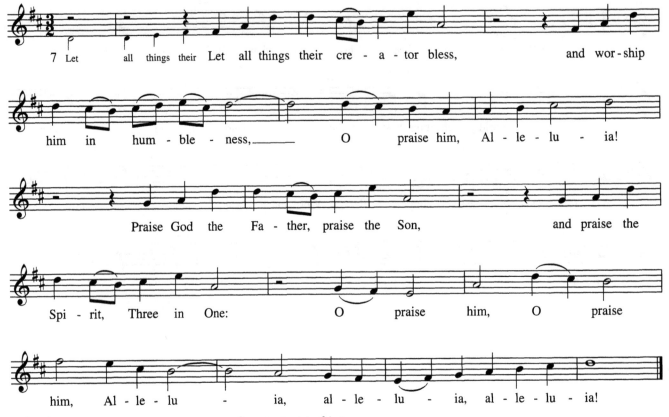

7 Let all things their Let all things their cre - a - tor bless, and wor - ship

him in hum - ble - ness,_____ O praise him, Al - le - lu - ia!

Praise God the Fa - ther, praise the Son, and praise the

Spi - rit, Three in One: O praise him, O praise

him, Al - le - lu - ia, al - le - lu - ia, al - le - lu - ia!

*This descant may accompany any stanza of any text set to this tune

Lasst uns erfreuen

melody from *Auserlesene Catholische Geistliche Kirchengeseng*, 1623

400 All creatures of our God and King, stanza 7

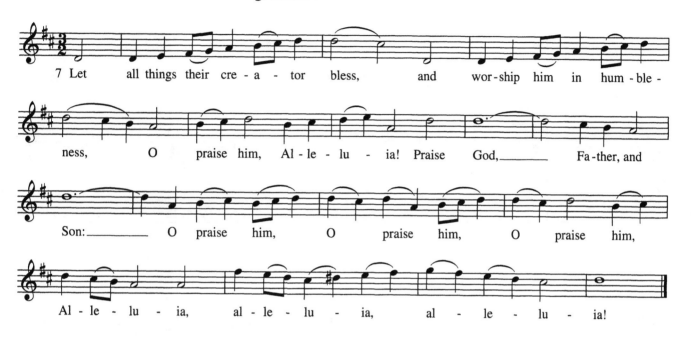

7 Let all things their cre - a - tor bless, and wor-ship him in hum - ble -

ness, O praise him, Al - le - lu - ia! Praise God,_____ Fa -ther, and

Son:_____ O praise him, O praise him, O praise him,

Al - le - lu - ia, al - le - lu - ia, al - le - lu - ia!

Lasst uns erfreuen

melody from *Auserlesene Catholische Geistliche Kirchengeseng*, 1623

618 Ye watchers and ye holy ones, stanza 4

4 O friends, in glad-ness let us sing,_____ an-thems ech-o-ing, Al-le-lu-ia. To God the Fa-ther, God the Son, and God the Spi-rit, Three in One. Al-le-

Words: John Athelstan Laurie Riley (1858-1945) © Oxford University Press. Used by Permission. All rights reserved.
Desc. and harm.: Thaddeus P. Cavuoti © 1999 Thaddeus P. Cavuoti. Used by permission. All rights reserved.

Words: John Athelstan Laurie Riley (1858-1945) © Oxford University Press. Used by Permission. All rights reserved.
Desc. and harm.: Thaddeus P. Cavuoti © 1999 Thaddeus P. Cavuoti. Used by permission. All rights reserved.

Laudes Domini

Joseph Barnby (1838-1896)

427 When morning gilds the skies, stanza 4

Words: German, ca. 1800; tr. Robert Seymour Bridges (1844-1930), alt.
Descant: William Bradley Roberts © 2004 William Bradley Roberts. Used by permission. All rights reserved.

Words: German, ca. 1800; tr. Robert Seymour Bridges (1844-1930), alt.
Descant: William Bradley Roberts © 2004 William Bradley Roberts. Used by permission. All rights reserved.

Laudes Domini

Joseph Barnby (1838-1896)

427 When morning gilds the skies, stanza 4

4 Sing, suns and stars of space, sing, ye that see his face, sing Jesus Christ be praised! God's whole creation o'er, both now and evermore shall Jesus Christ be praised!

May also be played by trumpets in C.

Words: German, ca. 1800; tr. Robert Seymour Bridges (1844-1930), alt.
Descant: William Bradley Roberts © 2004 William Bradley Roberts. Used by permission. All rights reserved.

Le Cénacle

Joseph Gelineau (b. 1920)

696 By gracious powers so wonderfully sheltered, stanza 4

4 Yet when again in this same world you give us the joy we had, the bright-ness of your Sun, we shall re-mem we shall re-mem-ber all the days we lived through, whole life shall our life shall be yours a-lone.

This descant reflects the conviction that descants need not be exclusively the province of grand hymns. With a light, lyric sound, perhaps only by one singer, a quiet descant might prove an effective complement to a subtle hymn.

Words: F. Pratt Green (1903-2000) © 1974 Hope Publishing Company, Carol Stream, IL 60188.
Descant: William Bradley Roberts © 1988 William Bradley Roberts. Used by permission. All rights reserved.

Leoni

Hebrew melody

401 The God of Abraham praise, stanza 5

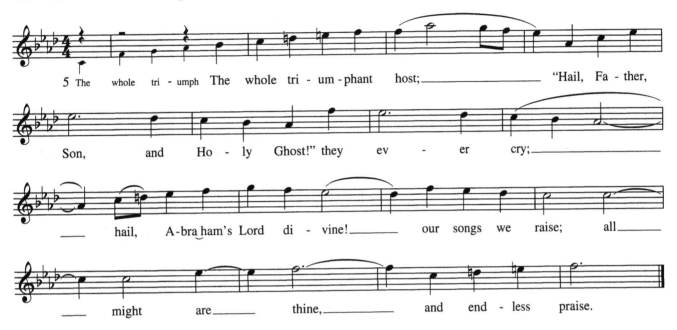

5 The whole tri - umph The whole tri - um - phant host;_____ "Hail, Fa - ther,

Son, and Ho - ly Ghost!" they ev - er cry;_____

____ hail, A - bra ham's Lord di - vine!_____ our songs we raise; all_____

____ might are_____ thine,_____ and end - less praise.

Words: Thomas Olivers (1725-1799), alt.
Descant: Harold Friedell © 1996 Pine Hill Press. Used by permission. All rights reserved.

Lux eoi

Arthur Seymour Sullivan (1842-1900)

191 Alleluia, alleluia! Hearts and voices heavenward raise, stanza 5

5 Al - le - lu - ia, al - le - lu - ia! Glo - ry be to God on high;

Al - le - lu - ia! to the Sa - vior has won the vic - to - ry;

Al - le - lu - ia! to the Spi - rit, fount of love and sanc - ti - ty:

Al - le - lu - ia, al - le - lu - ia! to the Tri - une Ma - je - sty.

Words: Christopher Wordsworth (1807-1885), alt.
Descant: Michael J. Dorio © 2004 Michael J. Dorio. Used by permission. All rights reserved.

Maryton

Henry Percy Smith (1825-1898)

660 O Master, let me walk with thee, stanza 4

4 In hope that In hope that sends a shin - ing
ray far down the fu - ture's broad - ening
way, in peace that thou canst give, with
thee, O Mas - ter let me live.

McKee

Afro-American spiritual

529 In Christ there is no East or West, stanza 3

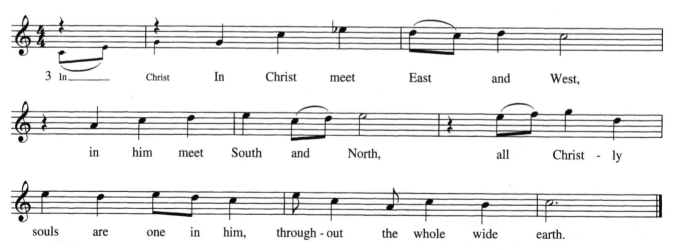

3 In_____ Christ In Christ meet East and West,
in him meet South and North, all Christ - ly
souls are one in him, through - out the whole wide earth.

Michael

Herbert Howells (1892-1983) © 1968 Novello & Co. Ltd.

665 All my hope on God is founded, stanza 5*

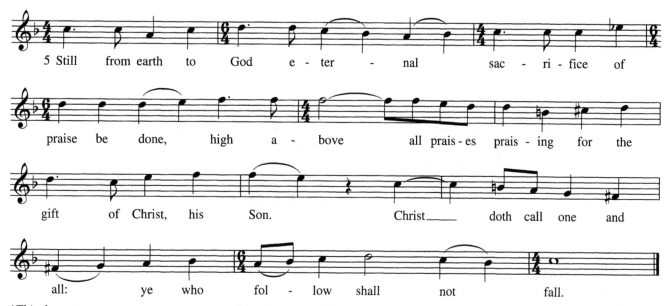

5 Still from earth to God e-ter - nal sac - ri - fice of
praise be done, high a - bove all prais-es prais-ing for the
gift of Christ, his Son. Christ____ doth call one and
all: ye who fol - low shall not fall.

This descant may accompany any stanza of any text set to this tune.

Words: Robert Seymour Bridges (1884-1930)
Descant: Charles Hogan © 2004 Charles Hogan. Used by permission. All rights reserved.

Michael

Herbert Howells (1892-1983) © 1968 Novello & Co, Ltd.

665 All my hope on God is founded, stanza 5

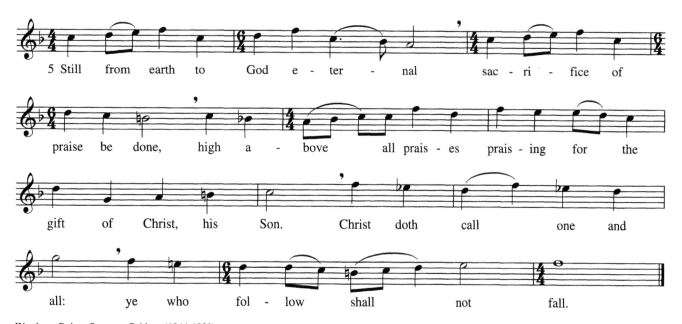

5 Still from earth to God e-ter - nal sac - ri - fice of
praise be done, high a - bove all prais - es prais - ing for the
gift of Christ, his Son. Christ doth call one and
all: ye who fol - low shall not fall.

Words: Robert Seymour Bridges (1844-1930)
Descant: William Bradley Roberts © 2002 William Bradley Roberts. Used by permission. All rights reserved.

55

Michael

Herbert Howells (1892-1983) © 1968 Novello & Co, Ltd.

665 All my hope on God is founded, stanza 5

5 Still from earth to God e - ter - nal sac - ri - fice of praise be done, high a -
bove all prais - es prais - ing for the gift of Christ, his Son. Christ
doth call one and all:___ ye who fol - low shall not fall.

Words: Robert Seymour Bridges (1844-1930)
Desc. and harm.: Thaddeus P. Cavuoti © 1998 Thaddeus P. Cavuoti. Used by permission. All rights reserved.

Mit Freuden zart

Melody from "Une pastourelle gentille," 1529

598 Lord Christ, when first thou cam'st to earth, stanza 4

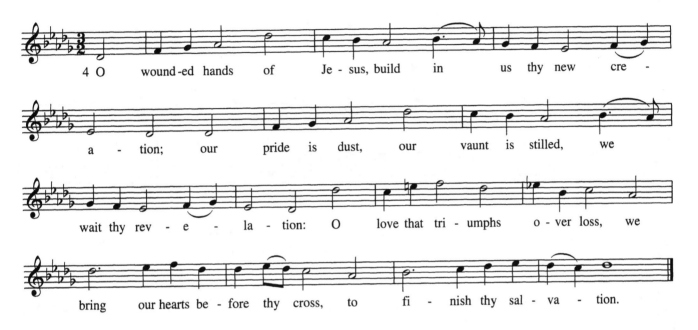

4 O wound-ed hands of Je - sus, build in us thy new cre -
a - tion; our pride is dust, our vaunt is stilled, we
wait thy rev - e - la - tion: O love that tri - umphs o - ver loss, we
bring our hearts be - fore thy cross, to fi - nish thy sal - va - tion.

Morning Star

James Proctor Harding (1850-1911)

117 Brightest and best of the stars of the morning, stanza 5

5 Bright - est _____ of the stars of the morn - ing,

dawn on our dark - ness, and lead us thine

aid; star of the hor - i - zon a - dorn - ing,

guide where our in - fant Re - deem - er is laid.

Words: Reginald Heber (1783-1826), alt.
Desc. and harm.: Richard R. Webster © 2002 Richard R. Webster. Used by permission. All rights reserved.

Moscow

Felice de Giardini (1716-1796)

365 Come, thou almighty King, stanza 4
371 Thou, whose almighty word, stanza 4
537 Christ for the world we sing, stanza 4

365 4 To Thee, great   One   in   Three,   the high - est   prais - es   be,
371 4 Ho - ly   and   bless - èd   Three,   glo - ri - ous   Trin - i - ty,
537 4 Christ for the   world   we   sing!   The world to   Christ   we   bring

hence ev - er - more;   thy sov - ereign ma - jes - ty   may we   in
wis - dom, love,   might;   bound - less   as   o - cean tide,   roll - ing   in
with   joy - ful   song;   the   new - born   souls, whose days,   re - claimed from

glo - ry   see,   and   to   e - ter - ni - ty   love and a - dore.
full - est   pride, through the   world,   far   and wide,   let there   be   light!
er - ror's   ways,   in - spired with   hope   and praise,   to   Christ be - long.

Words: (365) Anon, ca. 1757, alt.; (371) John Marriott (1780-1825), alt.; (537) Samuel Wolcott (1813-1886)
Descant: William D. Gudger © 1991 William D. Gudger. Used by permission. All rights reserved.

National Hymn

George William Warren (1828-1902)

718 God of our fathers, whose almighty hand, stanza 4

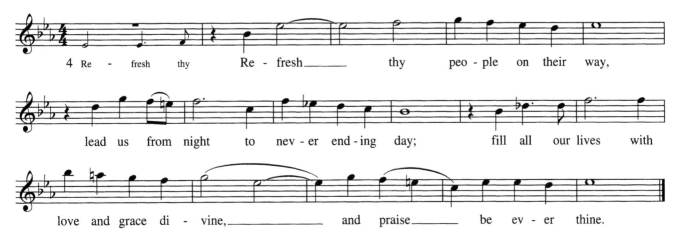

4 Re - fresh thy   Re - fresh_____ thy   peo - ple on their way,

lead us from night   to nev - er end - ing day;   fill all our lives   with

love and grace di - vine,_____ and praise_____ be ev - er thine.

Words: Daniel Crane Roberts (1841-1907)
Descant: Harold Friedell © 1996 Pine Hill Press. Used by permission. All rights reserved.

59

Nettleton

Melody from *A Repository of Sacred Music, Part II*, 1813

686 Come, thou fount, stanza 3

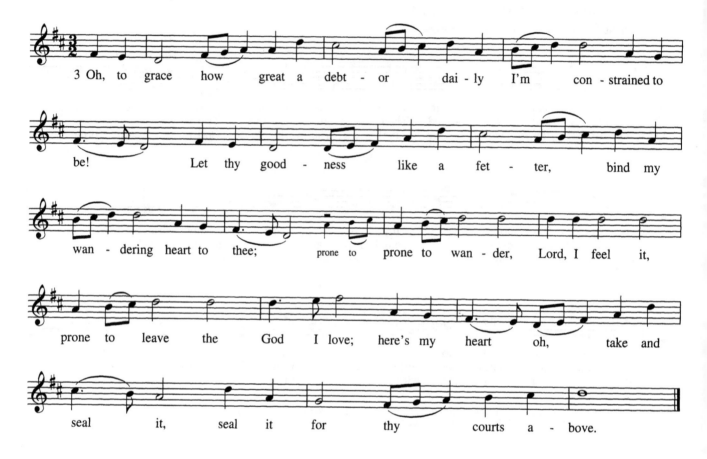

3 Oh, to grace how great a debt - or dai - ly I'm con - strained to be! Let thy good - ness like a fet - ter, bind my wan - dering heart to thee; prone to prone to wan - der, Lord, I feel it, prone to leave the God I love; here's my heart oh, take and seal it, seal it for thy courts a - bove.

Words: Robert Robinson (1735-1790), alt.
Descant: William Bradley Roberts © 2003 William Bradley Roberts. Used by permission. All rights reserved.

Newman

Richard Runciman Terry (1865-1938)

446 Praise to the Holiest in the height, stanza 5

5 Praise to the Ho - liest in the height, and in the
depth be praise; in all his words most
won - der - ful, most sure in all his ways!

Words: John Henry Newman (1801-1890), alt.

Nicaea

John Bacchus Dykes (1823-1876)

362 Holy, holy, holy! Lord God Almighty, stanza 4

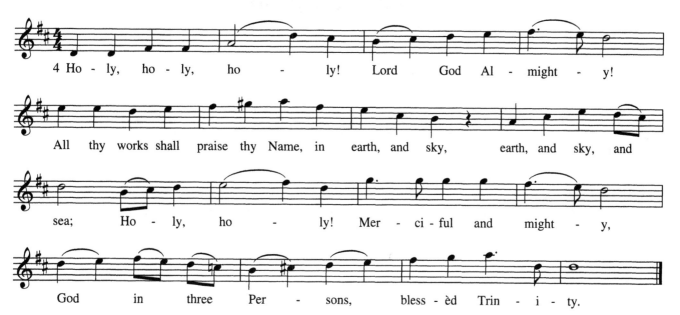

4 Ho - ly, ho - ly, ho - ly! Lord God Al - might - y!
All thy works shall praise thy Name, in earth, and sky, earth, and sky, and
sea; Ho - ly, ho - ly! Mer - ci - ful and might - y,
God in three Per - sons, bless - èd Trin - i - ty.

Words: Reginald Heber (1783-1826), alt.

Nicaea

John Bacchus Dykes (1823-1876)

362 Holy, holy, holy! Lord God Almighty, stanza 4

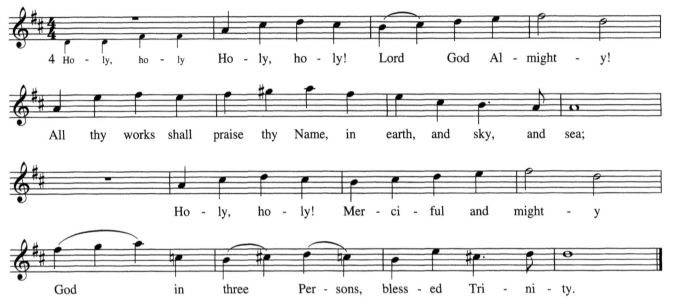

Words: Reginald Heber (1783-1826), alt.
Descant: William D. Gudger © 1984 William D. Gudger. Used by permission. All rights reserved.

Northampton

Charles John King (1859-1934) from *Hymns Ancient and Modern, Ltd.* (admin. Hope Publishing)

426 Songs of praise the angels sang, stanza 6

Words: James Montgomery (1771-1854), alt.
Descant: Iain Quinn © 2004 Iain Quinn. Used by permission. All rights reserved.

Nyland

Finnish folk melody

232 By all your saints still striving, stanza 3
655 O Jesus, I have promised, stanza 3
778 *Wonder, Love, and Praise* We all are one in mission, stanza 4

232 3 Then let us praise the Fa - ther and wor - ship God the Son and
655 3 O Je - sus, thou hast prom - ised to all who fol - low thee, that
778 4 Now let us be u - nit - ed and let our song be heard. Now

sing to God the Spi - rit, e - ter - nal Three in One, till all the
where thou art in glo - ry there shall thy ser - vant be; and, Je - sus,
let us be a ves - sel for God's re - deem - ing Word. We all are

ran - somed num - ber who stand be - fore the throne a -
I have prom - ised to serve thee to the end; O
one in mis - sion, we all are one in call, our

scribe all power and glo - ry and praise to God a - lone.
give me grace to fol - low, my Mas - ter and my friend.
var - ied gifts u - nit - ed by Christ, the Lord of all.

Words: (232) Horatio Bolton Nelson (1823-1913); (655) John Ernest Bode (1816-1874), alt.;
         (778) Rusty Edwards (b. 1955) © 1986 Hope Publishing Company, Carol Stream, IL 60188. Used by permission. All rights reserved.
Descant: Larry D. Cook © 2001 Larry D. Cook. Used by permission. All rights reserved.

Nyland

Finnish folk melody

655 O Jesus, I have promised, stanza 3

Pleading Savior

Melody from *The Christian Lyre*, 1830

586 Jesus, thou divine Companion, stanza 3

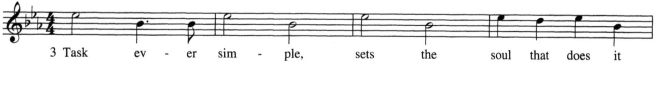

3 Task ev - er sim - ple, sets the soul that does it

free; ev - ery ev - ery deed of hu - man kind - ness done in love is done to thee.

Je - sus, thou Com - pan - ion, help us all to work our best; and

bless our dai - ly la - bor, lead us to our Sab - bath rest.

Alto voices may sing this descant taking lower pitches where provided.

Words: Henry Van Dyke (1852-1933), alt.
Descant: Thomas Pavlechko © 2004 Thomas Pavlechko. Used by permission. All rights reserved.

Puer nobis

Melody from Trier MS., 15th cent.

193 That Easter day with joy was bright, stanza 5

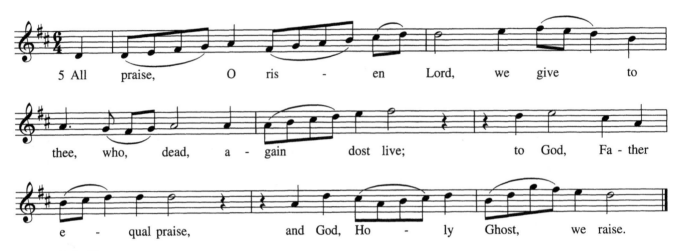

5 All praise, O ris - en Lord, we give to
thee, who, dead, a - gain dost live; to God, Fa - ther
e - qual praise, and God, Ho - ly Ghost, we raise.

Words: Latin, 5th c.
Descant: Albert Campbell © 2004 Albert Campbell. Used by permission. All rights reserved.

Raquel

Skinner Chávez-Melo (1944-1992) © 1985 Skinner Chávez-Melo

277 Sing of Mary, pure and lowly, stanza 3

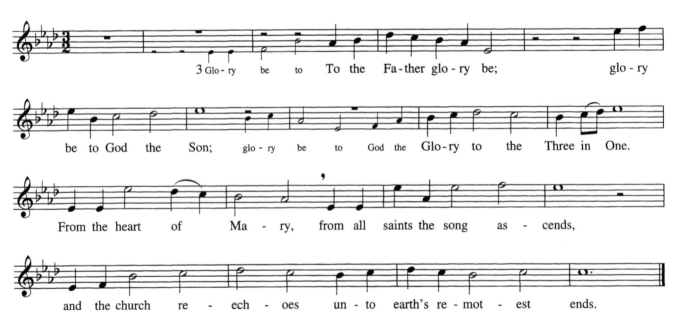

3 Glo - ry be to To the Fa - ther glo - ry be; glo - ry
be to God the Son; glo - ry be to God the Glo - ry to the Three in One.
From the heart of Ma - ry, from all saints the song as - cends,
and the church re - ech - oes un - to earth's re - mot - est ends.

Words: Roland Ford Palmer (1891-1985)
Descant: William Bradley Roberts © 1992 William Bradley Roberts. Used by permission. All rights reserved.

Richmond

Thomas Haweis (1734-1820)

212 Awake, arise, lift up your voice, stanza 5

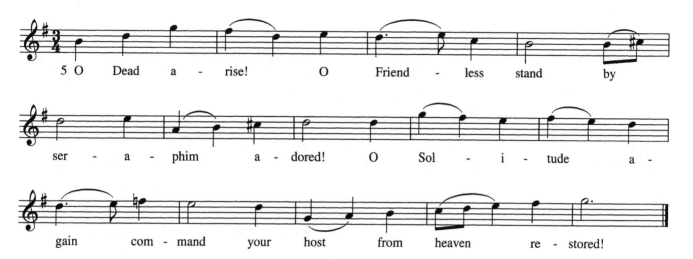

5 O Dead a - rise! O Friend - less stand by
ser - a - phim a - dored! O Sol - i - tude a -
gain com - mand your host from heaven re - stored!

Words: Christopher Smart (1722-1771), alt.
Descant: Iain Quinn © 2004 Iain Quinn. Used by permission. All rights reserved.

Rockingham

Melody from *Second Supplement to Psalmody in Miniature*, ca. 1780

321 My God, thy table now is spread, stanza 4
474 When I survey the wondrous cross, stanza 4

321   4 Nor   let   thy   Gos - pel   rest
474   4 The realm   of   na - ture mine,

till   the   world   thy   truth   has   run,   till
were   an   of - fering   far   too   small;   love

with   this   Bread   shall   all   be   blessed,   who
so   a - maz - ing,   so   di - vine,   de -

see   the   light   or   my   feel   the   sun.
mands   my   soul,   life,   my   all.

Words: Isaac Watts (1674-1748), alt.
Desc. and harm.: Richard R. Webster © 1990 Richard R. Webster. Used by permission. All rights reserved.

Rockville

Thaddeus P. Cavuoti (b. 1955) © 2004 Thaddeus P. Cavuoti

884 *Wonder, Love, and Praise* O all ye works of God, stanza 5

5 O let his peo-ple bless the Lord like right-eous souls of yore; let those of ho-ly, hum-ble heart come praise____ him ev - er - more.

St. Agnes

John Bacchus Dykes (1823-1876)

343 Shepherd of souls, stanza 4
510 Come, Holy Spirit, heavenly Dove, stanza 4

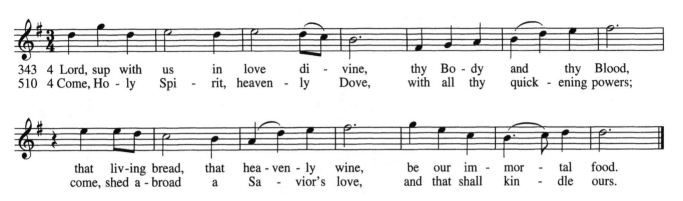

343 4 Lord, sup with us in love di - vine, thy Bo - dy and thy Blood,
510 4 Come, Ho - ly Spi - rit, heaven - ly Dove, with all thy quick - ening powers;

that liv-ing bread, that hea - ven - ly wine, be our im - mor - tal food.
come, shed a - broad a Sa - vior's love, and that shall kin - dle ours.

Words: (343) James Montgomery (1771-1854), alt.; (510) Isaac Watts (1674-1748), alt.
Descant: Iain Quinn © 2004Iain Quinn. Used by permission. All rights reserved.

St. Anne

Melody att. William Croft (1678-1727)

680 O God, our help in ages past, stanza 6

6 O God, our help in a - ges past, our

hope for years to come, be thou our guide while

life shall last, and our e - ter - nal home.

Words: Isaac Watts (1674-1748), alt.
Descant: Peter Crisafulli © 1989 Peter Crisafulli. Used by permission. All rights reserved.

St. Botolph

Gordon Slater (1896-1979) © Oxford University Press

209 We walk by faith, and not by sight, stanza 4*

4 That, when our life of faith is done, in
realms of clear - er light we may be - hold you
as you are, with full and end - less, end - less sight.

This descant may accompany any stanza of any text set to this tune.

St. Botolph

Gordon Slater (1896-1979) © Oxford University Press

209 We walk by faith, and not by sight, stanza 4

4 That when our life of faith is done, in
realms of clear - er light we may be - hold you
as you are, with full and end - less sight.

Words: Henry Alford (1810-1871), alt.
Desc. and harm.: Peter Crisafulli © 2002 Peter Crisafulli. Used by permission. All rights reserved.

St. Clement

Clement Cottevill Scholefield (1839-1904)

24   The day thou gavest, Lord, is ended, stanza 4

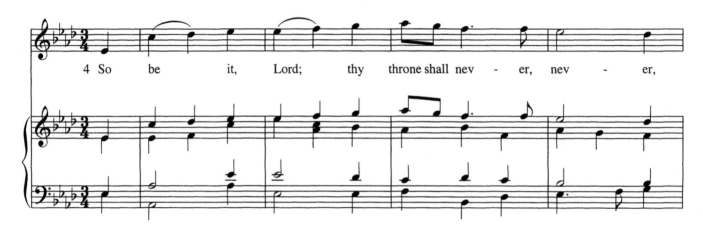

4 So be it, Lord; thy throne shall nev - er, nev - er,

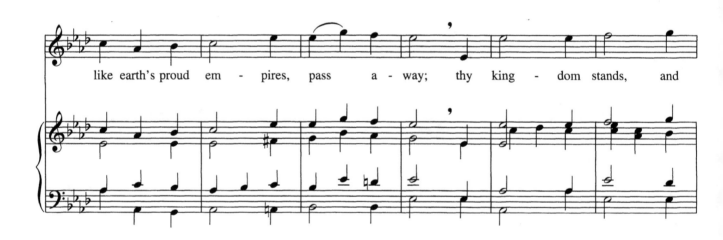

like earth's proud em - pires, pass a - way; thy king - dom stands, and

grows for ev - er, till all thy crea - tures own thy sway.

Words: John Ellerton (1826-1893)
Desc. and harm.: Richard R. Webster © 1987 Richard R. Webster. Used by permission. All rights reserved.

St. Clement

Clement Cottevill Scholefield (1839-1904)

24   The day thou gavest, Lord, is ended, stanza 4

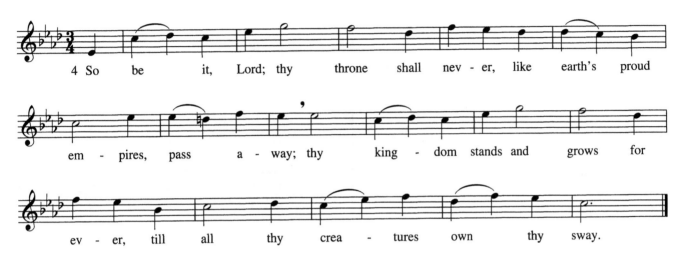

4 So be it, Lord; thy throne shall nev - er, like earth's proud

em - pires, pass a - way; thy king - dom stands and grows for

ev - er, till all thy crea - tures own thy sway.

Words: John Ellerton (1826-1893)
Descant: Douglas C. Shambo II © 1998 Douglas C. Shambo II. Used by permission. All rights reserved.

St. Columba

Irish melody

645 The King of love my shepherd is, stanza 6

6 And so through all the length of days_____ it nev - er fail - eth: Good Shep - herd, may_____ I sing thy praise with - in thy house for ev - er.

Words: Henry Williams Baker (1821-1877)
Desc. and harm.: Richard R. Webster © 1990 Richard R. Webster. Used by permission. All rights reserved.

St. Columba

Irish melody

645 The King of love my shepherd is, stanza 6

6 And so through all the length of days thy good - ness

fail - eth nev - er: Good Shep - herd, may I

sing thy praise with - in thy house for ev - er.

Words: Henry Williams Baker (1821-1877)
Descant: Gordon King © 1995 Gordon King. Used by permission. All rights reserved.

St. Columba

Irish melody

645 The King of love my shepherd is, stanza 6

Words: Henry Williams Baker (1821-1877)
Desc. and harm.: Thaddeus P. Cavuoti © 1995 Thaddeus P. Cavuoti. Used by permission. All rights reserved.

St. Columba

Irish melody

645 The King of love my shepherd is, stanza 6

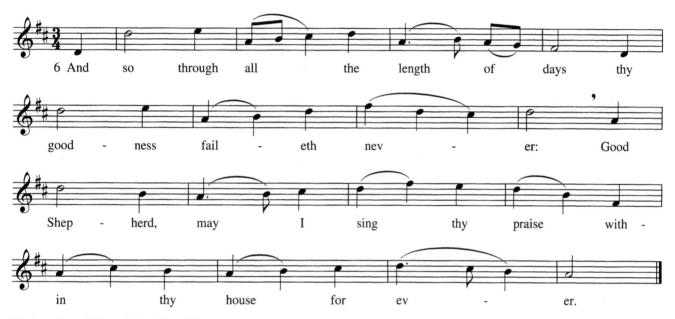

6 And so through all the length of days thy
good - ness fail - eth nev - er: Good
Shep - herd, may I sing thy praise with -
in thy house for ev - er.

St. Mark's, Berkeley

Irish melody from *Dante De: Hymns of God, Ancient and Modern*

69   What is the crying at Jordan, stanza 4

4 Now comes the day of sal - va - tion, in joy and ter - ror the Word is born!
God gives him - self in - to our lives; O dawn!____

St. Matthew

from *Supplement to the New Version of Psalms* by Dr. Brady and Mr. Tate, 1708

567 Thine arm, O Lord, in days of old, stanza 3

3 Be thou our great de - liv - erer still, thou Lord of life and death; re-
store and quick - en, soothe and bless, with thine al - might - y breath: to
hands that work and eyes that see, give wis - dom's heaven - ly lore, that
whole and sick, and weak and strong, may praise thee ev - er - more.

Words: Edward Hayes Plumptre (1821-1891), alt.
Desc. and harm.: Peter Crisafulli © 2003 Peter Crisafulli. Used by permission. All rights reserved.

St. Thomas

melody att. John Francis Wade (1711-1786)

58 Lo! he comes, with clouds descending, stanza 4

4 Yea, a - men! let all a - dore thee, high on thine e - ter - nal throne;

Sa - vior, take the power and glo - ry; claim the king - dom for thine own:

Al - le - lu - ia! Al - le - lu - ia! Thou shalt reign, and thou a - lone.

Words: Charles Wesley (1707-1788)
Descant: William Bradley Roberts © 2003 William Bradley Roberts. Used by permission. All rights reserved.

St. Thomas

melody att. John Francis Wade (1711-1786)

58 Lo! he comes, with clouds descending, stanza 4

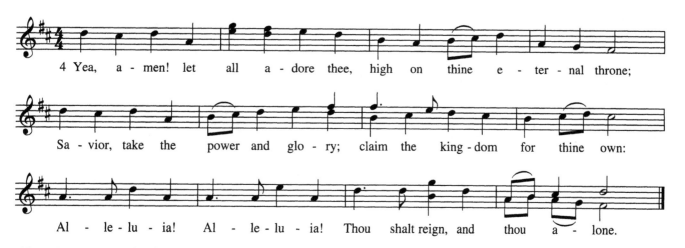

4 Yea, a - men! let all a - dore thee, high on thine e - ter - nal throne;

Sa - vior, take the power and glo - ry; claim the king - dom for thine own:

Al - le - lu - ia! Al - le - lu - ia! Thou shalt reign, and thou a - lone.

Alto voices may sing this descant taking lower pitches where provided.

Words: Charles Wesley (1707-1788)
Descant: Thomas Pavlechko © 2004 Thomas Pavlechko. Used by permission. All rights reserved.

Salve festa dies

Ralph Vaughan Williams (1872-1958) © Oxford University Press

175 Hail thee, festival day!, refrain

Hail thee, fest - i - val day! blest day that art hal - lowed for - ev - er, day

where - on Christ a - rose, break-ing the king - dom of death.
(of)

Lower parts are optional.

Words: Venantius Honorius Fortunatus (540?-600?); tr. *The English Hymnal*, 1906, alt. © Oxford University Press.
Used by permission. All rights reserved.
Descant: Douglas C. Shambo II © 1998 Douglas C. Shambo II. Used by permission. All rights reserved.

Salve festa dies

Ralph Vaughan Williams (1872-1958) © Oxford University Press

175, 216, 225 Hail thee, festival day!, refrain

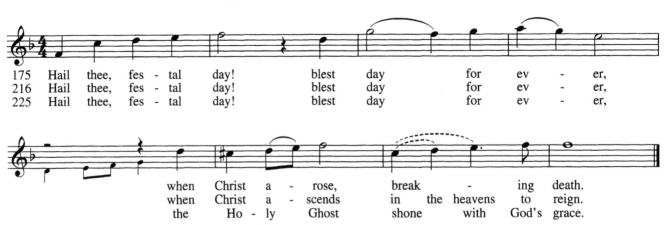

175	Hail	thee,	fes - tal	day!	blest	day	for	ev - er,
216	Hail	thee,	fes - tal	day!	blest	day	for	ev - er,
225	Hail	thee,	fes - tal	day!	blest	day	for	ev - er,

when Christ a - rose, break - ing death.
when Christ a - scends in the heavens to reign.
the Ho - ly Ghost shone with God's grace.

Words: Venantius Honorius Fortunatus (540?-600?); tr. *The English Hymnal*, 1906, alt.
Descant: Paul M. Ellison © 1995 Paul M. Ellison. Used by permission. All rights reserved.

Sine Nomine

Ralph Vaughan Williams © Oxford University Press

287 For all the saints, who from their labors rest, stanza 8

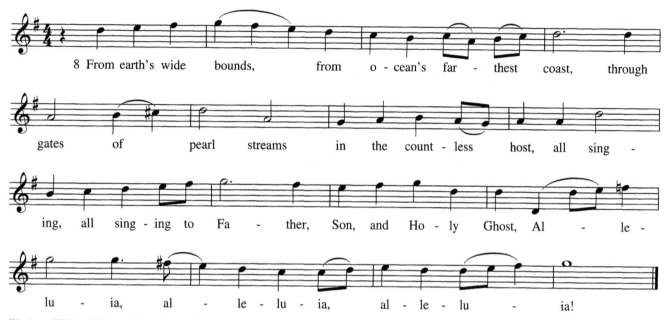

8 From earth's wide bounds, from o - cean's far - thest coast, through gates of pearl streams in the count - less host, all sing - ing, all sing - ing to Fa - ther, Son, and Ho - ly Ghost, Al - le - lu - ia, al - le - lu - ia, al - le - lu - ia!

Words: William Walsham How (1823-1897)
Descant: William Bradley Roberts © 2002 William Bradley Roberts. Used by permission. All rights reserved.

Sine Nomine

Ralph Vaughan Williams (1872-1958) © Oxford University Press

287 For all the saints, who from their labors rest, any stanza*

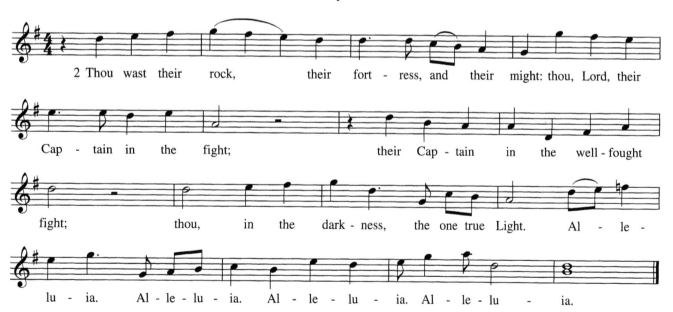

2 Thou wast their rock, their fort - ress, and their might: thou, Lord, their Cap - tain in the fight; their Cap - tain in the well - fought fight; thou, in the dark - ness, the one true Light. Al - le - lu - ia. Al - le - lu - ia. Al - le - lu - ia. Al - le - lu - ia.

This descant fits the standard Vaughan Williams harmony for any stanza. This text is used only as an example.

Words: William Walsham How (1823-1897)
Descant: Richard R. Webster © 1998 Richard R. Webster. Used by permission. All rights reserved.

Sine Nomine

Ralph Vaughan Williams © Oxford University Press

287 For all the saints, who from their labors rest, stanza 5 or 6

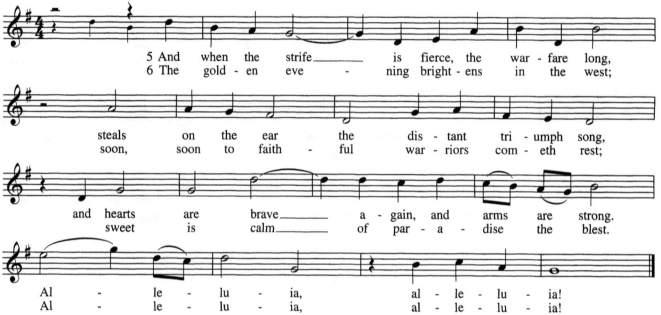

5 And when the strife___ is fierce, the war - fare long,
6 The gold - en eve - ning bright - ens in the west;

steals on the ear the dis - tant tri - umph song,
soon, soon to faith - ful war - riors com - eth rest;

and hearts are brave___ a - gain, and arms are strong.
sweet is calm___ of par - a - dise the blest.

Al - le - lu - ia, al - le - lu - ia!
Al - le - lu - ia, al - le - lu - ia!

Words: William Walsham How (1823-1897)
Descant: David G. Kelley © 2004 David G. Kelley. Used by permission. All rights reserved.

Sine Nomine

Ralph Vaughan Williams (1872-1958) © Oxford University Press

287 For all the saints, who from their labors rest, any stanza*

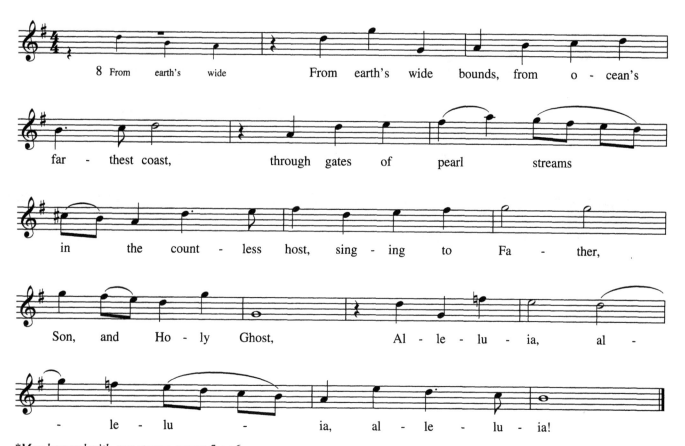

8 From earth's wide From earth's wide bounds, from o - cean's far - thest coast, through gates of pearl streams in the count - less host, sing - ing to Fa - ther, Son, and Ho - ly Ghost, Al - le - lu - ia, al - le - lu - ia, al - le - lu - ia!

*May be used with any stanza except 5 or 6.

Words: William Walsham How (1823-1897)
Descant: David G. Kelley © 2004 David G. Kelley. Used by permission. All rights reserved.

Siroë

George Frideric Handel (1685-1759)

546 Awake, my soul, stretch every nerve, stanza 4

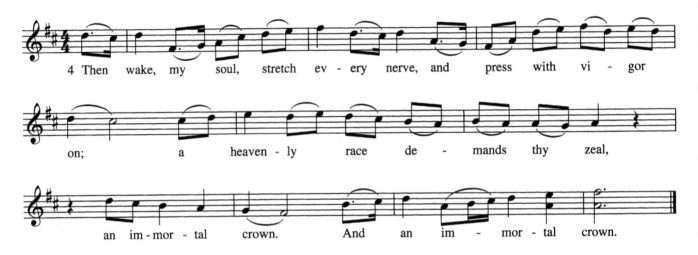

4 Then wake, my soul, stretch ev - ery nerve, and press with vi - gor

on; a heaven - ly race de - mands thy zeal,

an im - mor - tal crown. And an im - mor - tal crown.

Words: Philip Doddridge (1702-1751)
Descant: Albert Campbell © 2004 Albert Campbell. Used by permission. All rights reserved.

Solemnis haec festivitas

Melody from *Graduale*, 1685

120 The sinless on to Jordan came, stanza 6

6 On you may all your peo - ple feed, and know you

are the Bread in - deed, who gives e - ter - nal life to

those that with you died, and with you rose.

Sonne der Gerechtigkeit

Melody from *Bohemian Brethren, Kirchengeseng*, 1566

430 Come, O come, our voices raise, stanza 6

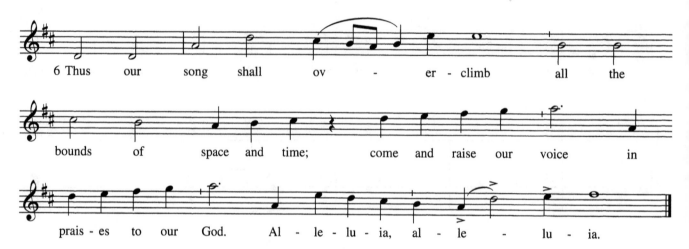

6 Thus our song shall ov - er - climb all the

bounds of space and time; come and raise our voice in

prais - es to our God. Al - le - lu - ia, al - le - lu - ia.

Words: George Wither (1588-1667), alt.
Descant: Jack Warren Burnam © 1990 Jack Warren Burnam. Used by permission. All rights reserved.

Stuttgart

Melody from *Psalmodia Sacra, oder Andrächtige und schöne Gesänge*, 1715

414 God, my King, thy might confessing, stanza 6

6 All   thy   works,   O_____   Lord,   shall   bless   thee;

King   shall   they   con - fess   thee,   and   pro - claim_____   thy   power.

Words: Richard Mant (1776-1848)
Desc. and harm.: Harold Friedell © 1996 Pine Hill Press. Used by permission. All rights reserved.

89

Stuttgart

Melody from *Psalmodia Sacra, oder Andächtige und Schöne Gesänge,* 1715

127 Earth has many a noble city, stanza 5

5 Je - sus, whom the Gen - tiles wor - shiped at thy glad e - piph - a - ny,

un - to thee, with God the Fa - ther and the Spir - it, glo - ry be.

Words: Marcus Aurelius Clemens Prudentius (348-410?). tr. *Hymns Ancient and Modern*, 1861, alt.
Desc. and harm.: Richard R. Webster © 2002 Richard R. Webster. Used by permission. All rights reserved.

Tysk

from *Psalm und Choralbuch*, 1719

475 God himself is with us, stanza 4

Words: Gerhardt Tersteegen (1697-1769); tr. Hymnal 1940, alt.
Desc. and harm.: Richard R. Webster © 1991 Richard R. Webster. Used by permission. All rights reserved.

Wareham

William Knapp (1698-1768)

137 O wondrous type! O vision fair, stanza 4

4 And faith - ful hearts are raised on high by this great

vi - sion's mys - ter - y; for which in joy - ful

strains we raise the voice of prayer, the hymn of praise.

Westminster Abbey

Henry Purcell (1659-1695)

518 Christ is made the sure foundation, stanza 4*

4 Here vouch - safe to all thy ser - vants_____ what they
ask of thee to gain; what they gain from thee,_____
____ for ev - er with the bless - ed to re -
tain, and here - af - ter in thy glo - ry
ev - er - more ev - er - more with thee to reign.

This descant may accompany any stanza of any text set to this tune. It may also be sung simultaneously with the descant printed in The Hymnal 1982 #518.

Words: Latin, ca. 7th c.; tr. *Hymns Ancient and Modern*, 1861
Descant: Charles Hogan © 2004 Charles Hogan. Used by permission. All rights reserved.

Zeuch mich, zeuch mich

Melody from *Geistreiches Gesang-buch*, 1698

286 Who are these like stars appearing, stanza 5

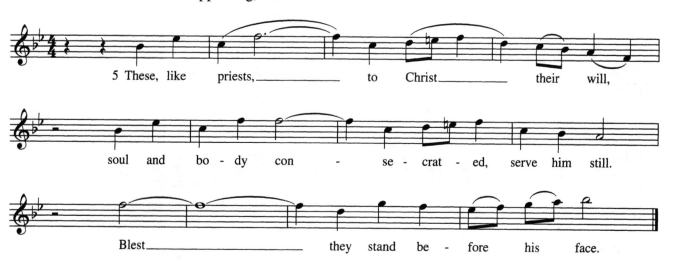

5 These, like priests,_____ to Christ_____ their will,

soul and bo - dy con - se - crat - ed, serve him still.

Blest_____ they stand be - fore his face.

Words: Theobald Heinrich Schenck (1656-1727); tr. Frances Elizabeth Cox (1812-1897), alt.
Descant: Harold Friedell © 1996 Pine Hill Press. Used by permission. All rights reserved.

Zion

Robert S. Lowry (1826-1899)

12 *Lift Every Voice and Sing* (We're Marching to Zion) Come, we that love the Lord, refrain

molto rit.

march - ing up - ward to Zi - on_____ the cit - y of God.

molto rit.

march - ing up - ward to Zi - on the beau - ti - ful cit - y of God.

molto rit.

Words: Isaac Watts (1674-1748)
Desc. and harm.: Carl MaultsBy © 2004 Malted Milk Music. Used by permission. All rights reserved.

INDEX OF FIRST LINES

INDEX OF COMPOSERS

Friedell,	Harold	Hyfrydol
		Lancashire
		Leoni
		Maryton
		National Hymn
		Stuttgart
		Zeuch mich, zeuch mich
Hogan,	Charles	Hyfrydol
		Michael
		Westminster Abbey
Kelley,	David	Dunedin
		Lasst uns erfreuen
		Sine Nomine
King,	Gordon	Antioch
		Coronation
		Diademata
		King's Weston
		St. Columba
MaultsBy,	Carl	Zion
Pavlechko,	Thomas	Grid
		Lambillotte
		Nicaea
		Pleading Savior
		St. Thomas
Quinn,	Iain	Newman
		Northampton
		Richmond
		St. Agnes
Roberts,	William Bradley	Abbot's Leigh
		Aberystwyth
		Antioch
		Aurelia
		Brother James' Air
		Cwm Rhondda
		Deus tuorus militum
		Down Ampney
		Duke Street
		Dunedin
		Earth and All Stars
		Engelberg

		Festal Song
		Lasst uns erfreuen
		Laudes Domini (2)
		Le Cénacle
		McKee
		Michael
		Nettleton
		Raquel
		Sine Nomine
		St. Thomas
Shambo II,	Douglas C.	Evening Hymn
		Hanover
		Hyfrydol
		Salve festa dies
		St. Clement
Stiller,	Susan	Forest Green
Webster,	Richard R.	Aberystwyth
		Bingham
		Birmingham
		Bromley
		Carlisle
		Down Ampney
		Gloria
		Morning Star
		Rockingham
		Sine Nomine
		St. Botolph
		St. Clement
		St. Columba
		Stuttgart
		Tysk

INDEX OF DESCANTS WITH ALTERNATE ACCOMPANIMENTS